Wedding

Hilarious Marriage Gags for yo

Compiled by Hugh

Montpelier Publishing
London
2014

ISBN-13:978-1505838008
ISBN-10:1505838002
Published by Montpelier Publishing, London.
Printed by Amazon Createspace.
This edition copyright © 2014. All rights reserved.
.

Prospective father-in-law to daughter's suitor: How much money do you have in the bank?

Suitor: I don't know. I haven't shaken it lately.

Jilly: I don't intend to be married until after I'm thirty.

Julie: And I don't intend to be thirty until after I'm married!

A man was watching a film at home and suddenly shouted at the man on the screen.

'Stop! Don't get out of the car, you're walking into a trap!'

'Are you watching a thriller, dear?' called his wife from the next room.

'No dear, just our wedding video'.

While on holiday in Egypt a man visited an ancient temple. He asked the guide what the big slab in the middle was for.

'That's the altar, where terrible sacrifices were made,' came the reply.

'Things haven't changed much,' said the man.

Losing a wife can be hard. In some cases, it's almost impossible.

'My wife doesn't understand me.'

'Maybe you just don't appreciate her enough?'

'No, she's a mail order bride and doesn't speak English'.

I took a vow of poverty and chastity. I didn't become a monk, I just got married!

An elderly man was in hospital with severe chest pains and his wife came to visit him.

'The doctors won't tell me anything,' said the man. 'Find out from them how bad it is, will you?'

The wife left the room, found a doctor and asked for the prognosis.

'He's in a bad way,' said the doctor, 'but there's a chance of recovery. If, and only if, you keep quiet around him, cook him good healthy food every night and have regular intercourse, he might just get better.'

The woman went back into the husband's room. 'What did he say?' asked the husband eagerly.

'He says you're going to die' replied the wife.

A man found that his credit card had been stolen but he decided not to report it because the thief was spending less than his wife did.

Wife: Let's go out tonight and have some fun.

Husband: OK, but if you're back before me, leave the hall light on!

After getting her boyfriend to reluctantly propose marriage, the young woman said 'Darling, you've agreed to marry me, but I still haven't heard you say those three very important little words...'

Confused, her boyfriend thought for a while then inspiration struck him.

'Is it mine?'

A man was on his deathbed after a heart attack and his wife sat by him.

He whispered, eyes full of tears, 'You have been with me all through the bad times. When I lost my job, you were there to support me. When my new business venture failed, you were there. When I became bankrupt, you were by my side. When we lost our house in that fire, you stuck by me. When my health started failing, you were still by my side...you know what?'

'What dear?' she gently asked, smiling as her heart began to fill with warmth.

'You're bad luck, get the hell away from me!'

Newsflash: Scientists have discovered a type of food which has been proven to put women off sex for life. It's called wedding cake.

Marriage: it begins when you sink in his arms. It ends with your arms in his sink!

There are two kinds of people at parties - those who want to go home early and those who want to be the last ones in the place. The trouble is that they're usually married to each other.

'My wife's an angel.'

'You're lucky. Mine's still alive.'

'My wife helped make me a millionaire.'

'That's great!'

'Not really. I was a billionaire before we met.'

'I can't keep the visitors from coming in,' said the office boy, dejectedly, to the chief executive. 'When I say you're out they just say they must see you.'

'Well,' said the chief executive, 'just tell them that's what they all say.'

That afternoon there called at the office a young lady. The boy assured her it was impossible to see the chief executive.

'But I'm his wife,' said the lady.

'Oh, that's what they all say,' said the boy.

My wife and I were blissfully happy for twenty five years. Then we met.

A man was in a cemetery, crying over a gravestone and saying over and over again, 'Why did you have to die? Oh, why did you have to die?'

A concerned passerby glanced at the name on the tombstone and asked 'What's the matter? Did your father die?'

'No.'

'Your brother, then?'

'No,' sniffed the man.

'Well, who died?'

'My wife's first husband.'

A Catholic priest preached a fine sermon on married life and its beauties. Two old Irishwomen were heard coming out of church commenting on the address.

''Tis a fine sermon his Reverence would be after giving us,' said one to the other.

'It is, indade,' was the quick reply, 'and I wish I knew as little about the matter as he does.'

The father of the bride caused a stir when he announced at the reception 'The bride and groom will be back in a minute. They have just gone upstairs to put their things together.'

My wife dresses to kill. She cooks the same way.

A lady rang up her husband's London club and asked to speak to him.

'Your husband isn't here, ma'am,' said the attendant, blandly.

'My goodness!' the lady exclaimed, 'How do you know my husband isn't at the club when I haven't even told you my name?'

The attendant answered more blandly than ever: 'Nobody's husband is ever at the club, ma'am.'

By all means marry; if you get a good wife, you will be happy. If you get a bad one, you will become a philosopher. *(Socrates)*

Many years ago a good for nothing fellow was up before the judge for being drunk and disorderly.

'Since this is not your first offence I sentence you to a month in prison with hard labour', said the judge.

'I demand clemency for my husband!' shouted the man's wife from the gallery.

The judge looked up angrily.

'Madam, one month is the minimum time your husband must serve in prison'.

'I'm not asking you to shorten the sentence, yeronner' replied the woman. 'I'm asking if he can do the hard labour at home instead.'

I never knew what real happiness was until I got married. By then it was too late!

The widow of a well-known man, requested that the words 'My sorrow is greater than I can bear' be placed upon the marble slab of her dear departed.

A few months later the lady returned and asked how much it would cost her to have the inscription removed and another substituted.

'No need of that, missus,' replied the mason, soothingly; 'you see, I left just enough room to add "alone."'

A man found an old lamp and rubbed it. A genie appeared and granted him one wish.

The man said 'I have always wanted to go to America but I am afraid of flying and also of boats. If only there was a road bridge between England and America, I could visit every week just by driving across.'

The genie thought for a few minutes and said, 'No, I don't think I can do that. It would be too much to ask. Do you have any other wish?'

The man thought for a minute and then told the genie, 'There is one other thing that I have always wanted. I would like to be able to understand women. What makes them laugh and cry, why are they temperamental, why are they so difficult to get along with? Basically, what makes them tick?'

The genie considered for a moment then said, 'So, do you want two lanes or four?'

A story is told of the nineteenth century author Mark Twain. When in Utah, a Mormon acquaintance argued with him on the subject of polygamy. After a long and rather heated debate, the Mormon finally said, 'Can you find for me a single passage of Scripture which forbids polygamy?'

'Certainly,' replied Twain. '"No man can serve two masters."'

A nagging wife finally drove her henpecked husband to an early grave. Feeling lonely with nobody to browbeat, she decided to try to contact her late spouse using a ouija board.

With trepidation in her voice, she asked 'are you there, Albert?'

After a pause, the glass moved and spelt out the message: 'YES'

'Are you in the next world?' asked the widow.

The answer came back. 'YES'

'And are you at peace?'

'YES'

The widow became increasingly curious and asked another question.

'Please tell me what Heaven looks like.'

Slowly the reply was spelt out.

'WHO SAID ANYTHING ABOUT HEAVEN?'

When a newly married couple smiles, everyone knows why.

When a ten-year married couple smiles, everyone wonders why.

In London's Highgate Cemetery there is a stone, erected by a widow to her loving husband, bearing this inscription: 'Rest in peace - until we meet again.'

Why do most men die before their wives? Because they want to.

'My wife took all my money and then left me.'

'You're lucky. My wife took all my money and she's still here!'

Marriage is an institution in which a man loses his bachelor's degree and the woman gets her master's.

Ugly woman (to annoying drunk): If you were my husband, I'd put poison in your tea.

Drunk: If you were my wife, I'd drink it!

'Before my wife and I were married,' said Smith, 'we made an agreement that I should have the final say in all major things, and my wife in all the minor.'

'How has it worked?' asked Jones.

Smith smiled. 'So far,' he replied, 'no major matters have come up.'

Nagging wife: 'Didn't I hear the clock strike two as you came in last night?'

Henpecked husband: 'You did, my dear. It started to strike ten, but I stopped it to keep it from waking you up.'

I got married to Miss Right. I just didn't realise her first name was 'Always'.

Husband: Fancy a quickie?

Wife: As opposed to what?

Woman to fiancé: When we're married I want to share all your troubles and worries.

Fiancé: But I don't have any troubles and worries.

Woman: I know, but we're not married yet.

A woman stood looking in the bedroom mirror. She was not happy with what she saw and said to her husband, 'I feel horrible; I look old, fat and ugly...I could really do with a compliment right now.'

The husband replied 'at least your eyesight is almost perfect.'

'I think my fiance's awful. I asked him if he had to choose between me and a million pounds, which he would take, and he said the million.'

'That's all right. He knew if he had the million you'd be easy.'

A married couple went out to a restaurant to celebrate their golden wedding anniversary. While driving home the wife saw a tear coming from her husband's eye.

'Are you crying because you're so happy that we have spent 50 splendid years together?' she asked.

'No,' replied the husband. 'I was just thinking about how your father threatened me that if I didn't marry you he would have me thrown in prison for 50 years. Tomorrow I would have been a free man!'

If a man's wife is his 'better half', does that mean there's nothing left of him if he remarries?

The curate was endeavouring to teach the significance of white to the children at morning service.

'Why,' said he, 'does a bride wear white at her wedding?'

As no one answered, he explained. 'White,' he said, 'stands for purity and joy, and the wedding-day is the most pure and joyous occasion of a woman's life.'

A small boy queried. 'Why do the men all wear black?'

A well-meaning florist was the cause of much embarrassment to a young man who was in love with a rich and beautiful girl.

It appears that one afternoon she informed the young man that the next day would be her birthday, whereupon the suitor remarked that he would the next morning send her some roses, one rose for each year.

That night he wrote a note to his florist, ordering the delivery of twenty roses for the young woman. The florist himself filled the order, and, thinking to improve on it, said to his assistant:

'Here's an order from young Mr Jones for twenty roses. He's one of my best customers, so I'll throw in ten more for good measure.'

Two women met at a business conference and one complained that her husband always came home late, no matter how she tried to stop him.

'Take my advice,' said the other woman, 'and do what I did. Once my husband came home at three o'clock in the morning, and from my bed, I called out "Is that you, John?" And after that he never came home late again.'

'But why?' exclaimed the first woman.

The other woman smiled. 'His name is Bill.'

A married man was having an affair with his secretary. One day, their passions overcame them and they checked in to a hotel. Exhausted from the afternoon's activities, they fell asleep and awoke at around 9 p.m.

The man dressed hurriedly but before he got home he rubbed his shoes in the mud on the front garden and made sure he got some grass stains on his trouser cuffs.

'Where have you been?' demanded his wife angrily when he entered the house.

'Darling,' replied the man, 'I can't lie to you. I've been having an affair with my secretary. I fell asleep with her in a hotel and didn't wake up until nine o'clock.'

The wife looked down at his shoes and said, 'You liar! You've been playing golf!'

'Jack and I have parted forever.'

'Good gracious! What does that mean?'

'Means that I'll get a huge bunch of flowers in about an hour.'

A man approached the very beautiful woman in the large supermarket and asked, 'Excuse me, I've lost my wife here in the supermarket. Can you talk to me for a few minutes?'

'Why?' asked the puzzled woman.

'Because every time I talk to a beautiful woman my wife appears out of nowhere.'

'Yes,' said the old man to his young visitor, 'I am proud of my girls, and would like to see them comfortably married, and as I have made a little money they will not go penniless to their husbands. There is Sophie, twenty-five years old, and a really good girl. I shall give her £10,000 when she marries. Then comes Caroline, who won't see thirty-five again, and I shall give her £30,000, and the man who takes Elizabeth, who is forty, will have £50,000 with her.'

The young man reflected for a moment and then inquired: 'You haven't one about fifty, have you?'

Father (to suitor): I won't have my daughter tied for life to some stupid fool.

Suitor: Then don't you think you'd better let me take her off your hands?

A woman marries a man expecting he will change, but he doesn't. A man marries a woman expecting that she won't change and she does.

A couple were walking through a picturesque village and came upon a wishing well. The husband leant over, made a wish and threw in a penny. The wife made a wish too, but she leant over too far, fell into the well, and drowned. The husband was stunned for a moment but then said, 'It really works!'

Married man: Cheer up! Plenty more fish in the sea.

Single man: Yes, but the last one took all my bait!

A couple were celebrating their golden wedding anniversary. The husband stood up and talked about the girls he knew in his youth. It seemed that every time he brought home a girl to meet his mother, his mother didn't like her. Finally, he started searching until he found a girl who not only looked like his mother and acted like his mother, she even sounded like his mother. So he brought her home one night to have dinner, and his father didn't like her.

A man put an advert in the Lonely Hearts column of the newspaper. All it said was 'Wife wanted.' Next day he received a hundred letters. They all said the same thing: 'You can have mine.'

What are the three things a woman likes most in a wedding service?

Aisle, altar, hymn. (I'll alter him).

Fortune teller: You wish to know about your future husband?

Lady: No; I wish to know about the past of my present husband for future use.

A depressed looking man walked into a bar. The bartender asked the man what was wrong. The man said 'My wife and I got into a huge argument, and she said she wouldn't talk to me for a month'.

The bartender said 'So what's wrong with that?'

The man replied. 'The month is up tonight'.

'Why have I never married?' the old bachelor said in reply to a leading question.

'Well, once upon a time, in a crowd, I trod on a lady's foot. She turned furiously, beginning, 'You clumsy idiot!'

Then she smiled sweetly and said, 'Oh, I beg your pardon! I thought you were my husband!'

Wife: Do you want a cup of tea?

Husband: Yes.

Wife: Yes *what*?

Husband: Yes, I do!

A woman's first husband was abusive. She got remarried and that husband deserted her. She got married again and that husband was hopeless in bed. Finally, she put an ad in the Lonely Hearts column of the newspaper: 'Looking for a man who won't abuse me, won't leave me, and won't fail me in bed.'

The next day, the doorbell rang and there on the step was a man with no arms and no legs.

'I saw your ad in the paper.' he said. I have no arms, so I can't hit you. I have no legs, so I can't run out on you.'

The woman thought for a moment about her requirements.

'How do I know you're good in bed?' she asked.

The man winked. 'I rang the doorbell, didn't I?'

Chauvinist husband (angrily): What! no supper ready? This is the absolute limit! I'm going to a restaurant.

Wife: Wait just five minutes.

Husband: Will it be ready then?

Wife: No, but then I'll go with you.

A couple had been married for 30 years and was celebrating the husband's 60th birthday. Their fairy godmother appeared and said she would grant them each one wish. The wife said 'I've never wanted much, but a new car would be nice.' The fairy waved her wand and in a puff of smoke a gleaming Rolls Royce appeared on their drive. Next, it was the husband's turn. He paused for a moment, and then said, 'Well, I'd like to be married to a woman 30 years younger than me.' The fairy waved her wand and with a puff of smoke, he became 90!

Two drunks were ambling homeward at an early hour, after being out nearly all night.

'Doesn't your wife miss you on these occasions?' asked one.

'Not often,' replied the other; 'she can throw pretty straight.'

Little Johnny: Daddy, how much does it cost to get married?

Father: I don't know, son, I'm still paying for it.

'What's the matter, old man? You look worried.'

'Well, to be honest with you, I am. You know, I took out some life insurance last Thursday.'

'Yes,' replied the sympathetic friend, 'but what has that to do with the worried expression on your face?'

'Well, the very next day my wife bought a new cook-book.'

A man was coming home late one night when a masked man burst out of his house, carrying a bag of stolen property. Fortunately a police car was passing just at that moment, and the burglar was apprehended.

The next day the man went to the local police station and asked to speak with the burglar.

'You'll get your chance in court,' said the policeman. 'What do you want to speak to him about anyway?'

The man replied. 'I want to know how he got into the house without waking my wife. I've been trying to do that for years!'

Two women were admiring each other's new clothing purchases. One showed off her new silk dress.

Fingering the fabric, she said, 'Just think, all this was made possible by a humble little worm.'

'I know,' said the other. 'I just wish *my* husband was as generous.'

A man and a woman who had never met before were booked into the same compartment on a sleeper train. After some initial mutual annoyance they both managed to get to sleep; the man on the top bunk, the woman on the lower. In the middle of the night the man leant over and said, 'I'm sorry to bother you but I'm awfully cold and I was wondering if you could possibly pass me another blanket.'

The woman looked up and with a gleam in her eye said, 'I've got a better idea...let's pretend we're married.'

'Why not!' said the man, enthusiastically.

'Good,' she replied. 'Get your own bloody blanket.'

'Do you act toward your wife as you did before you married her?'

'Exactly. I remember just how I used to act when I first fell in love with her. I used to lean over the fence in front of her house and gaze at her shadow on the curtain, afraid to go in.'

'And I act just the same way now when I get home late.'

'My wife is mourning the loss of a ten-thousand-pound diamond necklace.'

'Why don't you advertise a thousand pound reward and no questions asked? '

'Well, I could make good on the thousand, but I don't think my wife could keep to the rest of the deal.'

'What are you cutting out of the paper?'

'An item about a man getting a divorce because his wife went through his pockets.'

'What are you going to do with it?'

'Put it in my pocket.'

A man was on his deathbed.

'Grant me one last wish, my dear,' he gasped pitifully to his wife. 'Six months after I die I want you to marry Jones.'

'But I thought you hated Jones,' said his wife.

'I do,' said the man.

'Darling,' said the young married man, 'I have to go to Paris on business. It will only take a day or so and I hope you won't miss me too much while I'm gone, but...'

'I won't,' answered his young wife, positively, 'because I'm going with you,'

'I wish you could, dear, but it won't be convenient this time. What would you want to go for, anyhow? I'm going to be too busy to be with you.'

'I have to go. I need clothes.'

'But, darling — you can get all the clothes you want right here in London.'

'Thank you. That's all I wanted.'

My wife is temperamental. Fifty per cent temper and fifty per cent mental.

Mr. Brown: I had a strange dream last night, my dear. I thought I saw another man running off with you.

Mrs. Brown: And what did you say to him?

Mr. Brown: I asked him what he was running for.

'Now,' said the bridegroom to the bride, when they returned from their honeymoon trip, 'let us have a clear understanding before we settle down to married life. Are you the president or the vice-president of this society?'

'I want to be neither president nor vice-president,' she answered. 'I will be content with a subordinate position.'

'What position is that, my dear?'

'Treasurer.'

'My wife certainly makes my salary go a long way.'

'So does mine — so far that none of it ever comes back.'

Husband (newly married): 'Don't you think, love, if I were to smoke in the house, it would spoil the curtains?'

Wife: 'Ah, you are the most unselfish and thoughtful husband in the world; of course it would.'

Husband: 'Well, then, take the curtains down.'

My wife and I have agreed never to go to bed angry with one another. So far we've been up for three weeks.

The beautiful young woman interviewed a fortune-teller on the usual subjects.

'Lady,' said the clairvoyant, 'you will visit foreign lands, and the courts of kings and queens. You will conquer all rivals and marry the man of your choice. He will be tall and dark and aristocratic looking.'

'And young?' interrupted the lady.

'Yes, and very rich.'

The beautiful lady grasped the fortune teller's hands and pressed them hard.

'Thank you,' she said. 'Now tell me one thing more. How do I get rid of my present husband?'

Marriage is the process of finding out what kind of man your wife would have preferred.

Notice in a parish magazine: 'The Women's Institute will be holding a jumble sale this Saturday. A great chance to get rid of anything you don't want. Remember to bring your husbands.'

For every woman who makes a fool out of a man there is another woman who makes a man out of a fool.

A husband and wife were involved in a petty argument, both of them unwilling to admit they might be in error.

'I'll admit I'm wrong,' the wife told her husband in a conciliatory attempt, 'if you'll admit I'm right.'
He agreed and, like a gentleman, insisted she go first.

'I'm wrong,' she said.

With a twinkle in his eye, he responded, 'You're right!'

A policeman stopped a motorist speeding down a village high street.

'But officer,' the man said, 'I can explain—'

'Be quiet,' said the officer, and despite the man's protests arrested him and locked him in a cell at the police station.

A few hours later he brought the man a cup of tea. Again the man tried to speak but the constable told him to be quiet.

'You can explain it all to the magistrate in the morning. He'll be in a good mood when he gets back, it's his daughter's wedding today.'

'Don't count on it,' answered the motorist glumly. 'I'm the groom.'

A woman has the last word in any argument. Anything a man says after that is the beginning of a new argument.

Many people died in a big train crash and went up to the pearly gates of heaven. St Peter arrived and said, 'I want the men to form two queues. One for the men that dominated their women on earth and the other line for the men that were dominated by their women. Once that's done, all the women can come through with me for registration.'

After some time the women had gone through the gates and St Peter returned. There were two queues. The queue of the men that were dominated by their women was a mile long, but the queue of men that dominated their women contained only one man.

St Peter was angry. 'You men should be ashamed of yourselves. Look at you – there was only one of you strong enough to stand up to his wife. Tell them my son, how did you manage to be the only one in this queue?'

The man replied sheepishly.'I don't know, my wife told me to stand here.'

Little Johnny was at his first wedding. When it was over, he asked his mother, 'Why did the lady change her mind?'

'What do you mean?' asked his mother.

'Well,' replied Johnny, 'she went down the aisle with one man and came back with another.'

'So you want to marry my daughter, do you?' asked the girl's father of her young man.

'Very much indeed,' replied the youth.

'Can you support a family?'

The young man reflected a moment, and then asked. 'How many of you are there?'

Husband: I want to go somewhere on holiday this year I've never been before.

Wife: Well, how about the kitchen?

Marriage teaches you loyalty, meekness, forbearance, self-restraint, forgiveness - and a great many other qualities you wouldn't have needed if you'd stayed single.

A young man had been 'just friends' with a young lady. After a few months however he plucked up the courage to propose to her.

'Let's get married!' he said.

The young lady sighed. 'Who'd have us?'

What do you call a woman who knows where her husband is every night?

A widow.

After an argument, a wife said to her husband, 'You know, I was a fool when I married you.' The husband replied: 'Yes, dear, but I was in love and didn't notice it.'

What is the most effective way to remember your wedding anniversary? Forget it once.

A bride to be called her mother a few days before the wedding with some bad news.

'I've just found out that my fiancé's mother has bought the exact same dress as you to wear to the wedding.'

The bride's mother thought for a moment.

'Don't worry,' she said. 'I'll just buy another dress to wear to the ceremony.'

'But mother,' protested the bride, 'that dress cost a fortune. What will you do with it? It's such a waste not to use it.'

'Who said I won't use it?' her mother asked. 'I'll just wear it to the rehearsal dinner.'

After having concluded a time and motion study of a factory, an efficiency expert gave a warning to the factory's owner.

'Don't try these methods at home.'

'Why not?' asked the factory owner.

'I did a study of my wife's method of making breakfast,' explained the expert.

'She made several unnecessary trips between the fridge, cooker, table and cupboards, often carrying only one item. "Darling," I suggested, "why don't you try carrying several things at once?"'

'Did it save time?'

'Actually, yes. It used to take her 20 minutes to get breakfast. Now I do it in seven.'

He (cautiously): Would you say 'Yes' if I asked you to marry me?

She (still more cautiously): Would you ask me to marry you if I said I would say 'Yes' if you asked me to marry you?

Wife: Do you want dinner?

Husband: Sure, what are my choices?

Wife: Yes and no.

One Friday night, instead of going home, a man stayed out partying with the boys and spending his entire pay over the whole weekend.

When he finally appeared at home on Sunday night, he was confronted by his angry wife.

'How would you like it if you didn't see me for two or three days?' she asked.

He replied, 'That would be fine with me.'

Monday went by and he didn't see his wife.

Tuesday and Wednesday came and went with the same results.

On Thursday, the swelling went down just enough where he could see her a little out of the corner of his left eye.

In the first year of marriage, the man speaks and the woman listens.

In the second year, the woman speaks and the man listens.

In the third year, they both speak and the neighbours listen.

Husband to wife: Why do you keep reading our marriage licence?

Wife to husband: I'm looking for a loophole.

A cowboy, discovering his wife had been unfaithful, walked into a crowded saloon brandishing a revolver and yelled 'I'll kill whoever's been sleeping with my wife!'

A voice from the back of the bar shouted back, 'That's a six-shooter. You don't have enough bullets!'

'Does your husband remember your wedding anniversary?'

'No; so I remind him of it in January and June, and get two presents.'

I haven't spoken to my wife in 18 months. I don't like to interrupt her.

A man's wife was depressed so he took her to a psychiatrist. It wasn't long before the doctor realised what the problem was. He simply walked over to the woman, took her by the hands, looked at her in the eyes for a long time, then gathered her into his arms and gave her a big, warm hug. Immediately the woman looked happier.

The doctor said to the husband, 'See, that's all she needs.'

The man looked relieved and said 'That's great doctor. I'll bring her in Tuesdays and Thursdays each week, but I have to play golf on the other afternoons.'

My wife and I never argue. It's impossible since she's always right.

Smith and Jones were playing golf. As they were about to tee off, a funeral procession drove past them on the road by the golf course. Smith drew back from the ball, and touched the peak of his cap.

'That was a thoughtful gesture', said Jones.

'Well, it's the least I could do for my wife,' said Smith.

I live like a medieval knight. Every night I go to sleep with a battleaxe at my side.

My wife and I always compromise, I admit I'm wrong and she agrees with me.

Man is incomplete until he's married. Then he's finished.

A husband said to his wife, 'No, I don't hate your relatives. In fact, I like your mother-in-law better than I like mine.'

Little Johnny: Is it true, Dad, I heard that in some parts of Africa a man doesn't know his wife until he marries her?

Dad: That happens in most countries, son.

I take my wife everywhere, but she keeps finding her way back!

A wife went to the police station with her friend to report that her husband was missing. The policeman asked for a description.

She said, 'He's 35 years old, 6 foot 4, has dark eyes, a full head of dark hair, an athletic build, and is always smartly dressed.'

The friend protested, 'Your husband is 48, 5 foot 4, chubby, bald, and dresses like a slob!'

The wife replied, 'I know, but who wants HIM back?'

Our marriage is based on mutual respect. I respect my wife - and she respects that.

A man asked his wife what she'd like for her fortieth birthday.

'I'd like to be eight again,' she said, wistfully, looking at herself in the mirror.

So the next day, her birthday, he presented her with a huge Barbie doll, a big bag of sweets and two tickets to a fun fair.

'What's this rubbish?' snapped the wife.

'You said you wanted to be eight again, so I got you something suitable,' said the husband, feebly.

'I meant my dress size, you idiot!'

Smith: Every time I have a problem at work, I always look at the picture of my wife on the desk and it helps me get through it.'

Jones: That's great. Your wife must be a really wonderful woman.

Smith: Not really. I just look at her and think 'no problem can be worse than this.'

A man rushed home and shouted to his wife. 'Pack your bags, I've won the lottery!'

Excited about the prospect of an exotic holiday, the wife said 'What kind of clothes should I pack?'

'All of them, I'm kicking you out!'

She has her husband eating out of the palm of her hand – it saves on the washing-up.

The newlywed wife said to her husband when he returned from work, 'I have great news for you. What would you say if I told you there will soon be three in this house instead of two?'

Her husband ran to her with a smile on his face and delight in his eyes. He kissed his wife. 'Nothing would make me happier,' he said.

'That's good,' replied the wife, 'because my mother's moving in with us tomorrow.'

Make love, not war. Or if you want to do both – get married!

Other titles from Montpelier Publishing
Available from Amazon

Frugal living and moneysaving
1001 Ways to Save Money: thrifty tips for the fabulously frugal!
A Treasury of Thrift: save money with frugal wisdom from the past
The Men's Guide to Frugal Grooming
The Frugal Gentleman: classic style for less money

Body, mind and spirit
Non-Religious Wedding Readings
The Simple Living Companion
Non-Religious Funeral Readings
Spiritual Readings for Funerals
Marriage Advice: Dos and Don'ts for Husbands and Wives

Humour and puzzles
The Book of Church Jokes: a Collection of (Mostly) Clean Christian Chuckles
After Dinner Laughs: Jokes and Funny Stories for Speechmakers
After Dinner Laughs 2: More Jokes and Funny Stories
Scottish Jokes: a Wee Book of Clean Caledonian Chuckles
The Bumper Book of Riddles, Puzzles and Rhymes

Travel
The Dalai Lama Next Door: volunteering with Tibetans in McLeodganj
The Slow Bicycle Companion: inspirational quotes from cycling's golden age

Men's interest
The Pipe Smoker's Companion
Advice to Gentlemen
The Real Ale Companion
The Cigar Collection